Jesus Is Always Near!
Prayers to Help Children find God

Jane A. Bell

*All your children will be taught by God,
they will have great peace!*
Isaiah 54:13

Copyright © 2007 by Jane A. Bell

Jesus is Always Near!
by Jane A. Bell

Printed in the United States of America

ISBN-13: 978-1-60034-481-7
ISBN-10: 1-60034-481-X

All rights reserved solely by the author. The author guarantees all contents are original and do not infringe upon the legal rights of any other person or work. No part of this book may be reproduced in any form without the permission of the author. The views expressed in this book are not necessarily those of the publisher.

Unless otherwise indicated, Bible quotations are taken from the New International Reader's Version of the Bible. Copyright © 1995, 1996, 1998 by Zondervan.

The writer has tried to help unchurched readers get to the heart of God through paraphrasing some of the scriptures from *The Message* Bible and the New International Reader's Version to edify for simple understanding of the true message of God.

www.xulonpress.com

Dedication

This book is dedicated to all the children that are waiting for God to come and save them. It is dedicated to the children in my life that I know God has and is rescuing and using to rescue others.

Hold on, children, God is coming to set you free! Cry out! We the church need to hear your cries. We are listening and so is your Father in heaven who loves you! We are coming!

Love to Ed, Elizabeth, Sean, and Crystal, who are my heroes!

I thank God He has given me the pleasure of sharing our lives together in a family that He has designed.

Encouragement

I pray that as children and adults read through some of the promises of God found in this book they will meditate on them and believe that God is speaking to them directly and personally. God said He would teach our children and they would have great peace. I pray that this book would be a step in helping us all know the promises of God for the least of these, including our own.

I pray that this book would help children in desperate situations reach out to God and that He would begin to make His way's known to them. I pray that these children would continue to call out to God and hang on until He gets there.

I pray that the church would be strong and courageous and, as I have begun to do, go after the "least of these" with the spirit of comfort and healing and deliverance! I pray that this book would be given as a prophetic evangelistic tool and that God would pour out His love on anyone who picks it up, and that their spirit would supernaturally be touched and changed and healed by their Father in heaven who loves them with an unconditional, never-ending love.

I pray as God said in His Word that the last will be first and the first will be last. The children today who seem to be last in any or all situations in their lives will be the first in line to lead us all to heaven.

God sent His Son, who was abused, beaten, trampled, and made to suffer for the sins of others. Jesus was abandoned, and He has a lot in common with the hurting, abandoned, abused, and suffering children in society. God is gifting younger and younger children to minister for and to Him. Let us not look at the outrageous bad behaviors of children who are hurting. Let us look beyond that and know that these children are fighting for their lives. We need to look for the hidden things in these children and equip them for warfare. Then they will be set free to minister to and for God!

Jesus came so that **all could be saved!**

God's heart is with the children. You want to do the work that is on God's heart?

Hear the cries of hurting, emotionally, and physically sick children. Find children that society said are not worth the trouble, and go and minister healing! Wash them in the Word of God. In the powerful name of Jesus! See them set free.

Amen

God Has a Great Plan for You!
God has chosen you!

God wants you to help Him bring His love and power throughout the earth. We may never understand His complete love for us, and we may not understand how His power works in us, but He still wants to use us to bring His love and healing to the world.

God wants us to learn about Him and to tell others. As we get to know Him we will become strong in Him, and we will become full in Him. Then we will have His power to do what He wants.

God's great plan is for people who want to be strong and courageous and who will listen to Him. It is a plan that includes doing cool things for God.

You do not have to feel powerful, you just have to be willing and say yes. Tell God you are ready to help Him. He is the source of the power. We just have to be willing, say yes, and then listen and follow instructions.

We may not understand the *fullness* that God has for us. The best way to explain it is with God's Word, the truth. The book of Ephesians in the Bible explains *fullness* this way: **"When Jesus Christ lives in our**

heart we will have his power and His great love flow into us and through us to others....We may not understand it completely but we will be filled with everything that God has for us" (3:17,19).

Here are some things God would like us to start thinking about to begin doing His work here on earth:

Let's get geared for God.
He will give us full life, long life.
He will give us a fully satisfied life.
We should bring joy where there is sadness.
We should bring goodness where there is heartache.
We should bring peace where there is fighting.
We should bring healing to the sick.
We should pray for others when no one seems to care.
We should feed the hungry.
We should give water to the thirsty.
We should give clothes to those who need them.
We should be a friend to the friendless.
We should be a servant to others and not worry about how we feel.
We should tell others about His great love for everyone.

This is only the beginning of the things that are included in God's cool plan for you. As you get to know Him better He will show you a bigger plan for you!

God's plan is for the full power of His love to invade the earth.

God has chosen you to help spread the Good News!

That plan takes people who are willing to become strong and courageous! It takes people like you and me who will be brave and allow God to help them become all they can be.

Jesus is the ultimate example of how to live our lives. His life here on earth was all about rescuing people. He wants to rescue you and He wants you to help rescue others. Jesus wants you to join Him in rescuing the most desperate, hurting people.

How can you do that? You start by repenting and trusting Jesus. To repent is to turn from your sins. Ask Jesus to forgive them and then decide to stop doing them. To trust Jesus means that you obey Him. When you do this you are "born again" into His family.

Do you know what Jesus thinks about you? He thinks about you a lot. Every day. And He thinks about the wonderful creation He made in you! He dreams about you fulfilling the wonderful plans He has for you.

God knows that sometimes things are hard. He knows that sometimes you hurt. But He knows that life is more than feelings—feelings change a lot during life. One minute we are happy, the next someone makes us mad. Only God and His Word never change.

If we want to have the fullness of God we need to live above our feelings. This means that we do not want to do things just because we feel like it or not. Maybe God or our parents are asking us to do things and we don't feel like it. We know we should do the things we are asked to do, but for some reason we don't want to. Maybe we feel we are not capable. We must learn to obey God no matter how we feel.

God wants to help you fight through the junk in your life. The junk is all the bad stuff that is in our lives. The bad feelings, the bad stuff we have done, the bad stuff that has happened to us that is still hurting us. We want to start believing the good. Unfortunately, we easily fall for the enemy's lies. The enemy is Satan, the devil, but we'll just call him the enemy.

The enemy likes to throw our problems in our face so that they seem bigger than they are. The enemy wants us to believe the lies.

Instead, we must focus on God's promises for us.

The enemy cannot accuse you endlessly. He has to shut up when you know the promises. God's promises are your weapons to destroy the enemy. The promises force the enemy to back off. Use God's promises like a sword to force the enemy away.

The weapons, God's promises, are scattered throughout the Bible. Get to know the Bible very well. Read it all the time. That will help you defeat the enemy.

The enemy is all about stealing whatever he can from you. You name it, he will steal it.

He will steal the peace in your family. He will steal your health, your friends, your grades at school, your self-esteem. He will steal anything that is good in your life.

One of the most important promises you can remember is: *You can do all things when God helps you.*

God never insults you. He builds you up. He encourages. He corrects. But He doesn't tear you down.

That voice calling you stupid? Not God.

That voice that tries to steal hope from you? Not God.

That voice that keeps putting you down for something you've already confessed? Not God. The voice that calls you a loser? That is the enemy speaking.

God's voice is cheering you on, believing in you, pulling for you. God is the One who has a great plan for you. He will tell you how to accomplish this plan for Him.

Read His Word and you will get to know God's voice and plan.

That doesn't mean God is pleased with everything you do. Get to know the Bible and you will find out that He isn't thrilled when you dabble in lying and cheating, bitterness and jealousy, having sex, using drugs, impure language or thoughts, and slander. But you will also find out what He does enjoy, things like obedience, humility, compassion, mercy, and love.

It is not easy sometimes to know that God can and will help you do all things. You have to have faith. To have faith is to believe in something you cannot see. So stir up your faith by reading the Bible, and it will help you start believing more. He's with you even when you are afraid or nervous.

When you have accepted God's invitation to come into His family, He is with you as you take a difficult test, when you are the last one picked for teams, when you are home all by yourself and feeling lonely, when you are hurt and need comfort. He is there whenever you need a friend close by and when you need to make good choices. God is closer than the closest brother or friend could be.

Are You Ready?

So would you like to be someone who helps God accomplish His plan on earth? You can do it even though things may not look good now. You must start by believing. It is not going to be easy, but it is sure going to be worth it!

I know that some of our earthly fathers are not good examples for us. But for those of us who repent and trust Jesus, God becomes our Father. The perfect Father. When we call Him, He answers. Every good and perfect gift comes from Him. He delights in giving His little children good gifts!

Talk to God like you'd talk to a perfect father. You don't have to be ashamed or scared. Be honest with Him. If you're angry, express your anger. He can take it. He knows what is going on. And He wants what is best for you.

Those of us who belong to Him can call Him "Dad." He will not hurt us or leave us. He will never forget us.

If you learn the promises in the Bible and learn to speak with God, then you are on your way to having the fullness that God wants for you.

It is helpful to think about the promises often, especially when you hear the enemy talking in your ear. Remember, the enemy is the one who is saying that you are a loser. If you are feeling like a loser in any way, don't believe those thoughts. Get your weapons out, the promises from God in the Bible, and confront the enemy.

God has picked you, and you are not a loser! You are a winner when you stick with Jesus. Talk to Him often; He will encourage you.

I have enclosed some statements from the Bible that you can say out loud. This will help you tell the enemy that you know the promises of God, and the enemy will have to let you go. Sometimes the louder you say them the more helpful it is to believe. March if you want. Do whatever it takes. Sing and shout. Just get it out LOUD!

The Bible says that you can decree a thing and it will be established **(Job 22:28).** These declarations from the Bible- are true. As you declare them your faith will grow. Declare them for yourself and those you love. The truth will set you free. When you are free with God you are free forever.

Remember that Jesus is always near. It's one of the promises in the Bible. The Bible says that God will never leave those who belong to Him. "I will never, never, never leave you or forget you," says your Father, God.

The Bible is what you must believe! You must believe it over everything and everyone else. It is truer than what you think or feel. It is truer than what friends and family say. William Booth, the founder of the Salvation Army, describes the Bible this way: **"God has put His heart on paper."**

If you do not have a Bible, get one. Ask someone for one. If you do not have money to buy one or don't have one in your home, go to a church and ask for one.

Jesus is our example of how to live. He showed us how our full lives should be. He came to earth so that He could empower us to live in fullness. Get to know Him well.

Read the Bible and believe that what Jesus did you can do. Read the stories of Jesus' life, and do what He did and believe what He said.

Music is something that helps people connect with God. Listen to good music. Go to a music store and hook up with good Christian music. Find something you like. So, are you ready to move into your fullness with God?

Let's get started....

Here are some prayers according to some of the promises God has for us in His Word, the Bible. There are more promises at the end of this book. Pray these prayers for yourself and those you love. You can also use the promises in the back of the book to put into prayers or songs, or just repeat them until you memorize them. Then when you need to use them as your weapons you will have them right with you. You can use them to get the enemy off your back!

*God, Here I Am
I Choose You!*

*I*f you would like to have Jesus in your life and move with God into fullness, it is important to pray a prayer of forgiveness and ask God to be the boss of your life.

Here is a prayer to start.

A Prayer for Jesus to Be Boss of My Life

Dear Jesus, I would like You to be the boss of my life.

Please forgive me of all the things in my past that I have done wrong.

Help me to believe that You came to save me. Help me to trust You for everything. Fill me with all that You have for me. Give me Your strength and power and love so that I can live my life for You. Give me the fullness You have for me!

GO FOR IT... Go for fullness with God!

A Prayer to Know That Jesus Is Always Near

esus, You say that You will never leave me or forget me. I want to see You in every situation in my life. I need to see You at school, at home, and everywhere I go. I need to see You in everything I do. Jesus, thank You for saving me and not giving up on me. I know You will never give up on me.

I do not want to give up on myself. Help me to be strong.

Thank You, Jesus. You love me. Please speak to me and help me to know that You are always near.

The Bible says in the book called Hebrews [God speaking], **"I will not in any way fail you, or give up on you, or leave you without support. I will not, I will not, I will not in any way leave you helpless or forget you or let you down or relax my hold on you. I will hold you tight"** (13:5).

A Prayer to Know That God Has GREAT PLANS FOR ME!

esus, I want to believe that You have great plans for me! Help me to believe. I want to believe that what You say is true. Sometimes I have trouble doing the things I need to do, like my work at school. Please let me see some of the great plans You have for me now, even when I am young. I need to see some of the good things You have for me. I want to know that You can use me now. I want my life to count for something. I want this earth to be a better place because I am here. I want to have Your full plan for my life come to pass, for You. I want to live my life as You lived Yours on earth. I want to start now. Let me know Your ways. Show me the paths to take.

In Jeremiah 29:11 God says, **"I know the plans I have for you. They are plans for success, plans for good not evil. I have a plan for your future that includes hope."**

A Prayer to Help Me Believe Your Word

God, I want to know Your Word and the promises of Your Word. I want to learn the promises for me and all of what the Bible says. Help me to want to read the Bible. Help me to get a Bible somehow so that I can read it. Help me to want to put Your promises into practice in my life. Please change in me the things You would like to change. Change

me from the inside out. I want the full life You have for me. So change me in a way that lines up with Your plan for me and what You want me to be. I know that will not happen unless You change the things in my life that need to be changed. I will let You. I will trust You and obey You. I know when I make You happy and believe, it makes us closer. Then You can begin to show me the fullness of Your plan for my life. So I say YES to all You have for me. I say bring on the promises for me. Amen!
(Bring it on)

In 2 Corinthians 1:20, God says: **"I have made many great promises; the answer is yes to them all because of My great love for you and your love for Me. Say amen to the promises from Me."**

A Prayer for Forgiveness

Please help me to forgive those who have hurt me. Help me to ask for forgiveness of those I have hurt. I need to feel Your forgiveness. Help me, Father, to feel You close, to feel Your forgiveness. I want to help, not hurt, others. I want to help others become all they can be - like You want me to be, and I can be with Your promises for me. I want the fullness You have for me, and I want to help others receive their fullness in God. Help me to be kind and forgiving. Help me to do what I need to do to forgive and be forgiven. Help me to show You to others. Help me to show them the right things to do. God, I want to be like You – loving and kind.

In James 5:15, God says, **"Believe. Pray. I will heal you. If you have done wrong, ask for forgiveness and I will forgive you. You will be healed inside and out."**

A Prayer to Become Strong and Courageous

Strong and courageous? That is part of Your plan for me, to be strong and courageous for You. I don't feel strong and courageous. I certainly don't act strong and courageous. I want to be strong and courageous. Only You can help me, Lord. I say yes to You, Lord! I will be strong and courageous. Yes, I am willing!

Yes, I want to be like You, for You. I will not worry about how You are going to help me. I just say yes! I will look for You when I am nervous and scared. I will look for You whenever I need a close friend around. I will call to You and You will answer me. I will let You show me Your ways to become STRONG AND COURAGEOUS! I feel stronger and braver already... we are on the right road, Lord, because I have chosen You and You have chosen me. Thank You, Father.

In Joshua 1:9, God says, "**Strength! Courage! Give it all you have! Think about the promises of God day and night, making sure you practice them. Then you will get where you are going and you will succeed. Strength! Courage! Don't be timid. Don't get discouraged. I am with you; I am your God and I am with you every step you take.**"

A Prayer for No Stinkin' Thinkin'

God, I know that You insist I do not go along with the crowd. I do not always make the right choices. Help me to think about You and Your goodness, Father. Let the things out of my mouth be good things about You and others. I know that my words are important to You, and they can influence things for better or worse. My words begin in my thoughts. Give me good clean thoughts. Let my words bring encouragement to people and not bring them down. I want to show Your love to everyone I come in contact with. Help me to think on the things that are good and pure, not bad. Help me to get rid of the evil even when it starts in my own mind. Help me not to allow negative thoughts to stay in my mind. Fullness in God – that is what I want.

In 2 Corinthians 10:5, God says, **"Destroy all the reasons that keep you from knowing Me. Keep every thought under control. Change what you are thinking about when you have to, in order to make your thoughts obey Me completely."**

A Prayer for Obedience

Lord Jesus, I want to listen to You and follow Your directions to make You happy. I know that You like us to listen and follow directions. Sometimes it is hard to do the things You ask because I do not always understand how important it is to follow Your directions. To realize Your dreams for me, I need to be on the right road with You. I do not know what that road is right now, but You do. You know where I need to be in the fullness of Your plan and where I can help bring fullness to others. Help me to hear Your voice and know Your voice. Then help me to listen and follow directions. Speak to me, Lord. I am listening.

In John 10:3-5, God says, **"I will speak to you, and you will listen. I know your name and I will tell you where to go. I will go ahead of you and check out the way for you. You will follow me because you will know My voice. You will know the enemy's voice, and you will not follow the enemy's. Run from the enemy's voice and run to Me."**

A Prayer Against Fear

I am afraid a lot. I do not want to feel afraid, but I do. I know that fear does not come from You. I need to feel You in my life, God. I also know that even though I may feel afraid, You do not want me to give in to those feelings. Feelings can change; they are up and down. Feelings are not something I can count on. Your Word is stable and lasts forever. Everyone has feelings, but I will not live my life by my feelings. You would like me to do what You have asked me to do even though I may feel afraid. I trust You, God, even though it is hard. When You ask me to do something I will do it. There are many people I cannot trust. They have lied to me or hurt me, but You, God, I will trust. You are my heavenly Father who wants me to have a good life and will always speak the truth to me. If I am afraid I will trust that You will be with me. Don't let me down. I will try not to let You down. No fear!

In 2 Timothy 1:7, God says, **"I have not given you a spirit that will make you weak and fearful. I gave you a spirit that gives you power and love. It gives you the ability to love and be loved. It will help you control yourself."**

A Prayer Against Rejection

I feel alone, Lord. I am learning that You made me and You have a purpose for my life. I know You love me. I am desperate for You to save me. Help me to see myself as You see me, as part of Your great family. I know that You truly and totally accept me. Help me to not feel sorry for myself. Help me to do the best I can. Help me to know what love is really like, love that comes from You. Help me to show others the love that comes from You. Help me to accept

the love from people that want to love me, and not turn away. You will never leave me nor forget me. There are people that love me, let me remember them and You, when I am feeling alone. Even if others leave again, I know that they have loved me and I have loved them and it has been good. I will always have You. I will not give in to feeling badly. Thank You that You love me. Thank You that You made me. I love You, too!

In Psalm 27:9-10, God says, **"Do not turn your face from Me, even if you are hurting or angry. I have helped you. I will not leave you. Even though you may think your family has rejected you, I will not leave you. I will accept you and I will love you always. You and I together will be fine."**

A Prayer Because I Am Lonely

I feel all alone, Lord, but I am learning that You love me and are always with me. Lord, help me to understand that You truly love me and totally accept me just as I am. Help me to feel that You are here even when I am alone. Help me to understand that You will never leave me or forget me.

Help me to get to know You as my friend. Help me to know that You would like to do special things for me and that You are watching me all the time. You are smiling at me all the time, and I am smiling back. I want to bless You as You bless me, Jesus. Thank You, Lord.

In Numbers 6:24-25, God says, **"I will bless you, I will take good care of you. I will smile on you and be good to you. I will give you peace."**

A Prayer for When I Feel I Am Never Good Enough

There are so many times in my life when I feel like I am not as good as others. God, I am learning that You do not make mistakes. I have been made for a reason. I have been made so that You can love me. You have made me just the way I am. You made every part of me. You were watching when I was made in my mom's belly; You had Your eyes on me and have a plan for me. Help me to change the things You want to change about me, and help me not to worry about the things You think I should not worry about. Help me to know the difference.

Help me not to let the things I cannot control bother me, since I cannot control others. I can use my weapons, Your promises against the enemy, so that he has to back off. Help me to use self-control. Help me to know what is important to You. Help me to see myself the way You see me. I am Your special child, made to be like You.

Psalm 139:13,17-18 says, "I have created every part of you. I put you together in your mother's belly. You are amazing! I think about you in such great ways. You cannot count all the great thoughts I have about you. There are too many great thoughts to count, more than all the grains of sand at the beach."

A Prayer to Hear God's Voice

God, I would like to hear You speak to me. I hear voices talking to me already, but I want to know Your voice and do as You tell me. Please silence the voices that are not Yours. I want to be quick to do what You ask. Help me to read Your Bible because You speak to me as I read it. I need to hear the good things that You say about me. I know You won't talk to me like my friends do, but I can certainly hear You as I read Your Word. I want to know the steps to take in my life to have it count for something. I want to know the steps that will show me the way to You. I am listening, Lord. Please speak to me.

In Psalm 119:105-108, God says, **"My Word will show you the way. It is like a light that guides you. Take My promises to follow My ways. Praise Me freely - I love that! I will teach you the way to go!"**

A Prayer for Purity

God, it's me. I want to live a good clean life. I want to keep my body clean. I want to please You with the things I do with my body. Help me to guard my eyes. I will not look at things that will leave pictures in my mind that have a lasting negative impact. Help me to put things in my body that make me strong. Help me, Lord, to guard what I listen to. The things I listen to need to encourage me to reach the full plan of Your power and love flowing in me and through me to others. Help me keep my

feet on the path that You put in front of me. I will go where You tell me to go. I will not go where there is lots of trouble. I could get into trouble before I know it, and I don't want to do that. I can only do this with Your help. Help my hands to build things up, not break things up. Let my hands not touch things I should not touch. Help me to be creative. Feelings are strong at times, and I do not want to stir up feelings in me that might lead me to do something that would make You unhappy. I don't want to be pulled into something before I know it.

In Romans 6:12-13, God says, **"Let Me rule your body. Don't just do whatever you want - think about what I would like. Give Me your whole body; don't let your feelings rule. I will help you do the right thing and go only where I want you to go. Guard yourself from evil; guard your eyes, heart, hands, and feet. Guard your entire body from head to toe."**

*A Prayer That
I Am a Blessing!*

*I am a blessing to God! Yes I am!
God, it is amazing that I could be
a blessing to You. I would love You to bless
my friends and family. I would like to be a
blessing to them also. I would like them to see
Jesus in me. I am praying that my friends and
family would want to know You and love You.*

Please help me be strong. Help me to read my Bible every day. Help me to believe what I read. I want to believe Your Word. I know that someday I will be in heaven with You, and I want my friends and family to be with us together. When we get to heaven we will not have to worry about anything. Help me to believe. Help me to never quit talking to You.

"I am a special person to You, God...thank You! Your blessing will be on me! God will bless me in His strong name!" (Psalm 129:8).

"God will bless me with every spiritual blessing. Those blessings come from heaven. They belong to me because I belong to Jesus Christ. He decided long ago to adopt me as His child" (Ephesians 1:3-5).

I am made to be like GOD!

Thank You for making me to be just like You! Help me to use Your Word as You do—to bring Your plans to the earth. Let me say things that will bring goodness and healing and peace. I would still like You to be able to say about me: "It is good...very, very good!"

"God said let us make men and women like us. Let them rule the earth. So God created them in His image, to be like God. He blessed them and said it is good...very good!" (Genesis 1:26-27).

A Prayer to See the Power of God

$\mathcal{I}$ will go, Lord. I have said yes to You, so You are with me! You have given me power; I need that power to tell Your good news to the poor. I want them to hear it. You have given me power to heal the sick. I do want them to be healed! You have sent me to cheer up those who are depressed. I can't do this without Your power. You have sent me to share the freedom of Jesus for all people. Everyone needs Your love. You have given me power to take Your light into dark places so

that people will see You and be free from whatever is holding them back from freedom with You! Help me, God, to do these things! There are people who are counting on me to help them. Let me see people as You see them, and when You send them into my life help me to know exactly what You want to do for them.

"My Spirit is with you. I have given you power to tell the good news to the poor. You have been sent to comfort those whose hearts are broken. You have been sent to announce freedom for those who are held captive by the enemy. I want you to set prisoners free. I send you to set the captives free. I will be there with you in power" (Isaiah 61:1-3).

A Prayer for Healing

God, I need to be healed. I am sick a lot. I have learned about Jesus and His power to heal people. I also know that what He did we can do. I want to be healed. My prayers are powerful because I am praying Your Word and promises in the Bible. You say to use Your Word to make things better. So I say, Sicknesses leave in the name of Jesus and the promises He has for me! I say, I desire to be well and whole because Jesus died to set me free from sickness and disease. I believe I am healed because You have a great plan for me, and sickness is not part of that plan.

Jesus says, **"I tell you, when you pray for something, believe that you have already received it. Then it is yours"** (Mark 11:22-24).

"I took up your sickness and your sorrows, yet they considered Me forgotten by God. They thought it was God who forgot Me, His only Son; I was beaten for your sins. My body was crushed

for your wrongdoings. The torture that was done to Me came so that you would have peace. By the stripes that tore My back apart, and with My spilt blood on the ground, YOU ARE HEALED!" (Isaiah 53:4-5).

I Will Fight for Good

I see evil everywhere! People I love are doing things that are evil. I live here in this world, and I want to bring Your fullness to this world. I want to destroy the enemy. I want to use Your power through Your Word to get the enemy out of people's lives. Help me to love people with all my heart. Help me to love them but fight for their freedom with Your Word, God. Help me not to get confused about this. My fight is not with people but with Satan. I am a winner with You and my weapons! I will fight when people are hurt and need help; I will fight when evil is near. I will submit to God and pray the promises He has for me. I will believe God and His promises no matter what I think or feel. The weapons that make Satan back down are the promise in my Bible and the prayers of the Bible in my hand, I will fight!

"I do live in the world but I do not fight my battles the way the people in the world do. The weapons I fight with are not the weapons the world uses. My weapons have the power of God to destroy the enemy right where he lives. I do not fight with people. I use the Word of God to fight the evil powers that influence them"** (2 Corinthians 10:3-4).

These promises are what God wants you to believe about YOU! You can just say these as promises about yourself from God or about others. Maybe you could put these statements of your faith in prayers or songs. Or just think about the wonderful way God thinks about you!

Any way you do this, God will love it! This is the beginning to your fullness with God with power and peace. BELIEVE!

Here are Bible verses you could repeat or put into songs or statements of your faith in God and what He has for you. This will help build your faith. It will help you believe what our good God says about you!

I am a child of God! John 1:12

I am a friend to God; with Him I will be successful wherever I go. People see Jesus in me. This earth is a better place because I am here. God gives me what I ask for because He loves me. John 15:15

Jesus has chosen me to be His friend. He will use me with His power in me to heal people, to save the world, and to change the world for His good. John 15:16

God will speak to me. We will share our secrets. Jesus died so I can have a full, good life. I will live forever with my Father in heaven. That will be amazing! Romans 6:8

I will do only what God wants me to do. I will not do what I want but only what God wants. I will live forever with God. Romans 6:22

God is my Father. I can count on Him as a Father. He will take care of me. Romans 8:14; Galatians 3:26 and 4:6

I am connected with Jesus in everything. I will receive everything He has for me because He lives in me. Romans 8:17

Jesus lives in me. Every inch of my body has Jesus in it. What Jesus did on earth, I will do, because I want to be like Him and He calls me to be like Him. I believe Him more than I believe anyone else. 1 Corinthians 6:19

Jesus and the Holy Spirit will help me live my life successfully. We are living my life together. 1 Corinthians 5:17

Since Jesus now lives with me, I am a new person. I do not have to think or worry about all the junk from the past. I am free to be me, with Jesus. 2 Corinthians 5:17

I am part of God's family. The family of God is so big - it is spread all around the world. I never have to feel lonely. I want God to be pleased with what I do for Him. He sees my goodness. Ephesians 1:1; 1 Corinthians 1:2; Philippians 1:1

God planned me. I want to be like Him! He has a purpose for my life. The plan for my life was made a long time ago, before I was even thought of by my parents. I just need to listen and follow His direction. I will do the work He has for me to do. God wants me to have the excellent way for my life. Ephesians 2:10

God chose me! He loves me so much! God wants me just where I am to do His work. God gives me compassion, kindness, gentleness, and patience. He helps me think more of others than I do of myself. Colossians 3:12; 1 Thessalonians 1:4

I need to pay attention in my life. The enemy is not going to win. The enemy is trying to destroy me. He wants to chew me up and spit me out. God loves me and will take care of me. I hate evil and where it comes from. I will fight for what is right and do what is right. I will use my weapons, the promises of God, against the enemy so that he is destroyed in my life. There are people all over the earth cheering me on. 1 Peter 5:8

God gives me peace. He made peace.
1 Corinthians 14:33

I am more than a conqueror in all things through Jesus, who makes me strong.
Romans 8:37

Jesus is greater than all the problems in the world. Jesus helps me to overcome my problems. I do not have to worry about things because God is with me. John 16:33

There is freedom with God; God is with me, and therefore I am free. I will stand strong even when I do not feel brave because He is with me. Galatians 5:1

I have given everything I am worried about to Jesus, and He will take care of it for me.
1 Peter 5:7

Jesus is always near. He will never, never, never leave me or forget me. Matthew 28:20; Hebrews 13:5

Jesus is the greatest and He is in me. He is greater than the enemy, Satan, who is trying to take me out. God is greater and I am greater than the enemy because God is in me! 1 John 4:4

God will always show me the way to be successful. We are friends, and He goes ahead of me and shows me the way. He checks things out for me. I will follow Him. 2 Corinthians 2:14

Jesus has brought me through all the bad stuff in my past. I do not have to feel bad for the things I have done in my past or about my mistakes. He forgave me when I asked. Jesus loves me and I trust Him and we will go through life together. Galatians 3:14

I can do all things through Jesus, who helps me be strong. Philippians 4:13

I will not be afraid. The enemy wants me to be afraid, and even if I feel afraid I will not back down on what I should do. God gives me power and love. He wants me to love and be loved. He wants me to have self-control, and with His help I can do this. 2 Timothy 1:7

God, You are my strength! How wonderful You are! You give me Your fullness! Psalm 68:35

God, show me Your power! Show me Your strength! Do what You have done before. Psalm 68:28

God gives me wisdom - lots of wisdom - when I ask Jesus for it. Jesus, You know everything. So all I have to do is ask You for the answers. 1 Corinthians 1:3; James 1:5

I will remember God's loving kindness, His compassion and faithfulness. Jesus gives me hope. I do not need to be depressed about anything or feel sorry about things because Jesus is my hope forever. Lamentations 3:21-23

God is on my side! It does not matter who does not like me or pick me because Jesus is the King and He always picks me first! I will not feel sorry for myself. I am the special one because the King picked me first. Romans 8:31

Lord, let the words of my mouth and all my thoughts be pleasing in Your eyes. You are my rock and my Redeemer! Psalm 19:14

I will enter His presence by thanking Him for His goodness, and come into His presence by telling Him how wonderful He is! I will be thankful to Him and bless His name. He is good! His truth goes on forever and ever! Psalm 100:4-5

A Word to Spiritual Parents,

I would like to encourage you if you have influence over children, whether biological or not, to think outside the box. First, we all have children in our lives that may or may not be our biological children. Some of the children in our lives may be older, yet new in their relationship with the Father in heaven, so we have a responsibility to help them grow to all they are called to be in Christ.

This project was inspired by years of working with children who came into my life through adoption and foster care and realizing that these children needed to be washed in the Word of God so they could be delivered and set free.

Isaiah 54:13 says, "All your children will be taught by the Lord and great will be your children's peace."

I did not have peace in my house for a long time, but this was a promise I knew was true. I needed the peace God offered. The question was: How do I get it? I knew I needed to do the best I could to teach the children to rely on God, learn to hear His voice, and take His instruction, whether or not it made sense. Although I knew that trusting God was going to bring peace to these kids, I was desperate for it *now*! Sometimes it happened, despite my mistakes.

There are many children who can't hear us for many different reasons. Our children are being diagnosed with all sorts of mental illness. They are full of fear. They have attitudes that are large and strong. Yet through all this I believe that God can, and will, teach them.

The biggest part of the battle for the spirits of our children is accomplished by filling them with strong spiritual food. We may not see results right away, but children in crisis know they need help. They know that things are bad and they need a real answer to the crisis. The only answer is Jesus, through the Word of God.

I pray that this project will remind children that JESUS IS ALWAYS NEAR, that He has a great plan for them, that He loves them, and that there are adults who are willing to go to battle for their eternal purpose and for their freedom.

Children who are riddled with fear, anxiety, and torment need constant reminding that Jesus is always near. God has a plan of His fullness for these children; we need to carry the mats of kids everywhere to help them receive that from God.

I pray that this book can be adapted to children of all ages. In a perfect world all children are born into families with a loving mom and dad. These parents then teach the children about God, and the roots of the Word grow deep and strong.

Yet too often children are given up on and forgotten. Too many children in foster care are bouncing around the system. According to the U.S. Department of Health and Human Services statistics, as of 2004 there are 523,000 children in foster care in the United States. About 119, 000 are available to be adopted. Half a million kids are just getting their basic needs met and not much more. Each year more and more kids come into the system, but there are still not enough homes for all the children to be adopted!

Some children that are diagnosed with mental illness could be set free if someone administered healing and deliverance. If only someone could believe.

The Salvation Army is in a unique position. We have so many families and children that God is sending to us. Many of these kids are on the brink of disaster. They come to us in many different ways. Some come through our social services, some through our many programs for kids, and some through our after-school club programs. Sometimes they just wander in because there is no other place for them to go. There are so many kids in need!

We have the truth and they are desperately seeking the truth. God is leading many kids to us—how exciting! If we do what God calls us to do, share His truth and the promises He has for these children, they will be set free. Then they in turn will be the ones to go back to their troubled homes and help set their family members free! What an honor that God has placed on us for this ministry!

We are reminded in **Deuteronomy 31:12-14 which** in part says, *"Gather the men, women and children together. They can listen and learn to respect the Lord. They will be careful to obey all of the words of Your law.* **The children must hear it!** *They must learn to respect the Lord God. You are about to go across and take the land as your very own."* The children will take the promised land after they learn the laws. This is worth getting excited about!

Matthew 18 talks about the greatest in heaven - the ones like little children. Verse 7 ascribes woe to those who cause these children to sin. When God revealed this to me, my first thought was: *I would never cause a child to sin.* But what about the sin of omission? I may cause a child to sin because I give up on them or don't teach them the promises of God. I need to share all the promises of God even if I think the children cannot hear those promises for any reason. Some of the children have bad attitudes and act as if they do not want to hear. Some have emotional problems and are unable to hear. I cannot judge what they do or do not hear, but I trust that their spirit will receive the words whether I know it or not.

So I have learned to use the Word of God to wash the children in my life through music and memorizing Bible promises; I have the children write the promises into decrees and prayers. For example, Jeremiah 29:11 says that God has a great plan for me, to prosper me and give me a hope and a future. I ask the children to personalize that promise into their own prayer and statement of faith.

God speaks to people's spirit deep inside of them. As adults, we can learn through prayer and fasting to connect with God at that deep level. When we pray for our children, their flesh may not be responding to us, yet we must press on. We may be battling for their spirit. I have prayed the prayers in this book over many children and out loud with them. I have had them pray the prayers over each other and themselves. When children are not thinking the way God thinks about them I remind them of what He says about them in His Word. I try to use the Word to prophesy over them, even during difficult moments when things seem the darkest.

I encourage you to play music at bedtime—music that shares the love of God is soothing and will help bring in the peace of God. For some of my children this is a real cleansing time. They were fearful of the dark or bad dreams, and having the promises of God at bedtime did two things: the love of God washed away fear and doubt, and it erased all the negative things of the past in a loving, supernatural way. They experienced peace during their sleep. Do not underestimate the work God can do through music.

I heard of a child who was not necessarily focused on God, and neither were her foster parents. Yet when she was having a bad time and needed comfort, she wanted to hear Christmas music. When I heard that story I immediately knew God was releasing His love through the comfort of the story of Jesus, and it was reaching her spirit.

I also heard of a foster child burdened by a multitude of emotional problems compounded by the fact that her biological family could not or did not want to care for her. So her foster parents sent her to a Salvation Army camp. At this Christian camp, this young and very troubled "throwaway" kid said the best part of camp was when all the kids were singing. Again, the music was speaking to her spirit. God spoke to her broken spirit to bring peace and release His love to her.

Go through these prayers and learn to listen to God for more detailed plans for your family and the children you influence. But get started, one verse at a time. We need to be forceful at using the Word of God to get these kids cleansed and free—filling them with the love of God and freeing them from the oppression of the evil of their past and the hold it has on them.

During times when my kids needed "adjustments," I tried to teach the Word. If I could find a verse in the Bible that applied to the issue the children were dealing with, I would have them write it out in their own words, then put it into a prayer.

I was desperate. Desperate for God and the peace He promised.

Recently I read this verse in Deuteronomy 1:39

"The little one that you said would be taken captive, your children, who do not know good from bad—they will enter the land I will give them and they will take possession of it."

The ones we thought would be held captive will possess the Promised Land. That land is here on earth. The ones you look at and are almost ready to give up on, the ones you fear are too far gone—yes, those are the ones God is setting free and letting enter the Promised Land, with peace and prosperity and wholeness.

Be aggressive in speaking, teaching, and talking about the promises of God for you and your children. Your words are powerful. Use faith-filled words. Calling things as they should be even though we may not see it now.
Romans 4:17

Take the time to hear from God. Listen for His instruction on raising your children. He will make His ways known to you. Remember that He will make His ways known to your children also. Believe for you and yours.

Give the children opportunities to hear God speaking. Have conversations about what God is saying to your children. Be careful not to dismiss what they are hearing too quickly. Keep a journal. It may be helpful to look back on.

Keep your standards high for your children, especially the children with special needs of any kind. There are many professionals who would like to diagnose and label these children, but we are working for the God who heals and is above all. We are working for God almighty. Listen to Him above others. Do not dismiss the professionals, but remember that God is above all that.

Be strong and courageous!

God is a warrior, and He wants you to battle with Him for your kids. Go to your prayer closet and fight for your rights with God.

Your children will be mighty in the land.
Psalm 112:2

Another term for "mighty" is *heroes*. My heroes are my children and the children who have come from awful circumstances and allowed God to raise them up above the mess. They have sometimes gone through painful processes of looking at the junk in their lives, letting go of the past, and dealing with the evil that has come against them. They have chosen to allow God to heal them and become heroes themselves. God is bringing children into fullness much younger than ever before. He is also including young children that we thought would be lost.

This might be a long process. Be prepared! Do your best. God will fill in the blanks. Get plenty of rest when you need it, and stay obedient to God as He makes His ways known to you. Do not quit now—it is never too late to start speaking life and love over (and to) your kids. God is more than enough for us all.

I know a young boy who came into a foster home when he was three years old. He had been in four other homes and was considered uncontrollable. The foster mom was asked to keep this child for just two weeks until they found some sort of institutional setting for him. He was in diapers, could not talk, and did not walk very well. His biological mother and some of the people who worked with him thought he needed to be diagnosed as autistic or with another severe emotional label. Well, this foster mom kept this almost four-year-old for a couple of days and discovered that he was very stubborn but could follow instruction if he was sure his caretaker was strong enough to follow through.

Jesus is Always Near!

Two weeks was stretched to three, then four. The foster mom knew someone was in that brain and spirit that God wanted to release. The foster mom used to whisper in the child's ear: "Is anyone in there?" The young boy, of course, did not want anyone to touch him. He could not communicate.

Then one day while sitting on the couch this uncommunicative little boy, without touching the foster mom, tried to whisper in her ear: "Anyone in there?" Breakthrough. He was so close to her face that she could feel the warmth of his body.

Have you ever seen the movie about Helen Keller? Annie Sullivan is teaching Helen manners, and food is flying everywhere, but Helen is not allowed to eat unless she uses manners. Well, not all of us will be in those kinds of situations, but for this young boy and his foster mom it was pretty close. The situation was rough for some time in this family. When freedom comes, oh how sweet it is!

This boy is now in regular school. God has done a great healing, and this boy hears from God on a regular basis. One morning he woke and asked his now adopted mom: "Does God speak to you?" His mom replied, "Yes!" He tapped his chest and said, "In here?" His mom again replied, "Yes!"

The boy answered, "Well, God said He loves me."

WOW! What a revelation for this broken little boy!

The next day he got up again and said to his mom: "God spoke to me again." His mom asked what God had said, and the boy replied, as he tapped his chest again, "GOD HAS HEALED MY HEART!" Thank You, God. The mother was awestruck.

This is one of my heroes.

My last story is about a little girl. I met her when she was five. The abuse in her biological home was horrific. No foster family really wanted this child because she had vulgar language and she knew how to use it to offend people.

This young girl was so tormented by the enemy of her soul that she was almost not able to function in a family setting. The foster mom knew she had to enter the hell this girl was in to get her out into the light.

The uncontrollable rage went on for hours: swearing, fighting, and breaking things. When these rages were happening it usually took two adults to keep her from hurting herself or others. The foster mom stuck with it, barely. The home was often in an uproar. One day in the midst of rage, this child cried out, "Why was I ever born?" The foster parent said the first thing that came to mind: "God has great things planned for you, and He will give you a future with really great things that He wants you to do for Him."

What a shock this little girl had! God had a plan. Then the foster mom told the child that God liked to sing to His children. The child—completely naked, covered in sweat in a corner, and wrapped up in fear—asked what song God would sing to her. God inspired her foster mom with these words: "Jane, I love you Jane, oh yes I dooooo. I love you Jane, yahooo, I love you Jane, yahoooo, I love Janie yes I do."

The peace that flowed into that room was remarkable. Bedtime came swiftly, and one more battle was over.

After a few months of settling, the inspired foster mom confided to Jane that she was turning out to be a nice girl. An overjoyed Jane agreed. Her eyes flooded with five-year-old tears, overwhelmed that someone thought she was valuable.

I could tell many stories about many children who have become heroes. But it is time to close.

As I have said, not all of us are called to reach out to the "worst," but some of us are. There are 500,000 kids in foster care, and some of us do not feel the need or the call to step up to the plate and do God's work? Kids are counting on the church to be all it should be—bold, fighting for justice, and moving in powerful healing and deliverance ministries. The church needs to receive a strong "mother anointing" so that no child is left behind. Jesus came that all would be saved! God is with you and He will equip you. Don't turn away! This is going to be huge! There are so many children, and God is going to do something great and wonderful. I certainly don't want to miss anything! Step up and see all that God has for these kids and you! New families! Only God can come up with such a great plan!

For the ones that God has entrusted to us, for all the children, God is more than able to raise up heroes. Sometimes believing that is the hardest part. It is about what God has already done. We just have to believe the promises—and hang on!

Please pray this prayer with me:

Father, thank You that You entrust Your children to us here on earth. We are humbled that You entrust us with these little ones.

Too often, though, Lord, we have not done a good job in protecting the children. Father, we acknowledge that the children continue to cry out… we hear those cries. Too often we turn our backs on them.

We are standing in faith believing that all the promises in Your Word are true for all Your children. With our help, prayer, time, and energy, children will move closer to their fullness in You.

We announce that from this day forward we will not look away, and we will not cover our ears to drown out the cries. Instead we will run to You and receive the strategic plan for freedom for the children.

We know that this battle must be fought on our knees in prayer. We know that we must be in contact with You at all times, reading the Bible and listening to You.

While we are on our knees, we also know that we will be feeding the children, brushing teeth with the children, washing the children, and continually sharing the promises You have for them. We will be washing them with soap and water and with the Word of God, the promises we find in Your Word.

Help us to be creative when we work with older children. Please break their hearts so that they want to know You better. Help us to find ways to bring light to their souls, even though they may not know that they need or want Your light.

Help us be strong to share Your love, God. Fit all the pieces of Your message together with compas-

sion as You fix the broken hearts of the lost, broken children.

Lord, we cannot do this without You. We are amazed that You allow us to partner with You in sharing the message of Your love with those who do not know it. Lord, we want to make You happy in this. Please help us as we step out in faith to save the children.

We call on You, God, who is more than enough for us all. Please pour everything we need on us and through us.

Give us a vision of what the children can be. Give us the ability to be consistently strong in love, words, deeds, compassion, and kindness.

May Your kingdom come on earth as it is in heaven. You are a Father to the fatherless. Help us be the mothers and fathers to the children who have none, the children who need good examples of what parents are. You are creating families through a spiritual DNA that only You can create. Thank You, Father.

What a beautiful big happy family there will be in heaven as we bring all the children to You.

Amen!

About the Author

*J*ane Bell has witnessed miracles of faith and prayer right under her own roof, and right before the eyes of many Family Services, foster care, and public education professionals. The experts have declared limits over the children Jane has committed herself to care for, but the Lord is having the final word in the lives of these miracle children through Jane's deep faith in the promises of God found in Scripture, and through her daily diligence in the trenches of miracle-making in the lives of broken children. Anyone who comes anywhere near Jane and her growing family of walking miracles can see the joy of the Lord and devil-defying power of Jesus Christ in the least of these, the children.

Janet Munn
Territorial Ambassador for Prayer
and Spiritual Formation
The Salvation Army
USA East

Printed in the United States
76061LV00001B/268-315